INNER DOOR

POETRY

AME THYST

Made with ♥ on the Notion Press Platform
www.notionpress.com

I dedicate this book to all those who love poetry and see the reflection of life in it.

Contents

Contents

Contents

Foreword

This poetry collection is a tapestry woven from countless threads of inspiration, love, sorrow, reflection,and imagination. Each poem, shaped by a different theme, stands as a tribute to the emotions and experiences that make us human.

What makes this book stand out is not just the range of themes it covers, but the way each one is handled—with tenderness, wisdom, and a keen awareness of both the personal and the universal. Reading these poems feels like sitting across from an old friend, one who sees the world with fresh eyes and speaks in a voice uniquely their own. This collection is not just meant to be read—it is meant to be felt, pondered, and revisited. It is a journey worth taking, and I'm grateful to walk alongside you as we turn these pages together.

To write poetry is to bare one's soul—to gather the fragments of thought, emotion, memory, and silence, and craft them into something that resonates beyond the self. In this collection, [Author's Name] has done just that, presenting not only a body of work, but a living, breathing portrait of the inner world we all share in some way.

From the very first page, it becomes clear that this is not just a poetry book; it is a journey through the vast terrain of human experience. Each theme explored—whether love, loss, longing, resilience, faith, nature, or identity—carries with it a raw honesty and emotional depth that refuses to be ignored. The poems do not simply describe emotion; they evoke it, pulling the reader into moments that are as intimate as they are universal.

.There are books that entertain, some that teach, and then there are those rare books that open something within us—unlocking rooms we had forgotten, doors we were afraid to open, or windows we never noticed before. **"INNER DOOR"** is one such book. This remarkable collection of poetry invites the reader into a journey that is both deeply personal and profoundly universal.

True to its title **"INNER DOOR"** does not shy away from vulnerability. It walks through corridors of memory, grief, love, hope, identity, and transformation, pausing at every threshold to reflect, question, and ultimately, embrace what lies on the other side. Each poem stands as a door—some familiar, some mysterious, and others aching to be stepped through. And behind every one is an honest echo of the human spirit.

This book is a gift. A companion. A mirror. A set of keys for those moments when we feel locked out of our own hearts. Whether you are new to poetry or a lifelong lover of verse, you will find something here that opens you—gently, courageously, and with grace.

It is with deep respect and admiration that I write this foreword. Inner Doors is more than a collection of poems; it is a threshold. May you walk through it slowly and return to it often.

Qasim Kashmiri

Poet, Novelist

Acknowledgements

With heartfelt gratitude I would like to extent my warmest greetings to everyone who picks 'Inner Doors' as one of their books to read. **"INNER DOOR"** is a collection of poems written across time, each a key to rooms within the heart and mind. These pieces are my way of examining life's details—not just as they are, but as they feel. Passion, sorrow, wonder, and tranquillity to live here, because to me, poetry is how we name the unspoken.

Some poems were born from a single glance; others from years of untangling emotions. I hope they invite you to pause, to look closer, and to open your own Inner doors.

Special gratitude to Qasim Kashmiri my editors, mentors, and supporters whose encouragement helped these poems find their form. And to the readers: may you see your own reflections in these lines. Your valuable feedback to my debut work will be highly appreciated. I am looking forward to experience your insights towards this book.

Yours,

Amé Thyste.

Prologue

Everything is in colour

Except hearts,

Souls and love

About The Author

Enter Caption

Ame Thyst is a poet whose words weave delicate tapestries of emotion, culture, and inner introspection. With a pen that dances between the lyrical and the profound, she explores themes of love, identity, heritage, and the human experience. Painting in souvenirs, dreams or myths, Her poetry resonates with a rare authenticity, blending the richness of her roots with universal truths that speak to the soul and only to the souls.

Born with an innate sensitivity to the world around her, **"Hafida"** her real name" discovered the power of poetry early in life. Each verse she crafts is a testament to her journey—marked by resilience, beauty, and an unwavering passion for storytelling. Her work invites readers into intimate landscapes of thought, where every line carries the weight of whispered confessions and bold declarations.

Ame's writing is not merely an art form but a bridge—connecting hearts across languages, borders, and generations. Whether through the melancholy of lost moments or the euphoria of newfound love, her poetry leaves an indelible imprint on those who encounter it. When she is not lost in the world of words, Ame finds inspiration in nature, music, mythology and the silent stories of everyday life. She believes in poetry as a force of healing and transformation, a belief that shines through her evocative compositions.

Ame Thyst continues to enchant readers with her unique voice, one that is destined to linger in the literary world for years to come.

1. My Light, Existence, My Soul

Don't look into my eyes, please
I'm still there, trying to be
Dancing with my inner child
Hiding, playing without making noise
What you could find through your eyecup,
A place to browse my books, my life?
Or a blank page where you could point out your rage
I see you trying to scratch my old books
Every time you cross an act,
A scene you won't like
Don't look
I'm naked with my thoughts and all senses
I'm all what I could be if you look deep
If you could see
My light and all stars
My curves
My gloves and masks
My strength and dreams
My fog
My coffee on table
Cold or hot
If you would be me!

You won't start explaining
Why I keep my feathers
My crown
My blurry faces
I am,
A storm, a museum that has been
A warm pillow and large doors
A tiny dancer on a flute sounds
A chance, a cloud of your life
Don't look into my eyes
Don't be a mirror
So can't see through yours.

2. I Breath You

How could I make you breathe again
And inhale your suffocation?
Crack this world of fails
Someone to save
Scarfs to paint with my arms
Someone to face
Someone to change
Something to change
Redemption sings its lanes
Melody of love
Melody of faith and grace
I won't stop believing in you
When it's not me who created you
But some forces we know, but can't see
I'll keep you close after rain and storms
So your heart will never turn to stones
And your hope to make it work
For me is to see you breathe again.

3. How?

How loyal darkness can be
In my thoughts forced to see?
Limits of my courage I can't clear
Drawing cheapest red lips on
And I'm ready to go…

4. The Wisard Heart

I could see
even with eyes closed
time revealed
the sun always shining
I could hear
events and thoughts
upon heads
around hearts
All whispers are
moon-catchings
I could feel
light and skies,
stars and scarves,
calm and fights,
captions of flames
in movies or on stages,
tones of voices
The steps and knots
never lie
I could see ocean depths
if you let me!

INNER DOOR

5. Home

I want to go back to
where I can fly,
again
Walking feels heavy here
my body is laden
with thoughts, future and past
Everything is in colour
except hearts,
souls, and love
I am using words I don't mean;
listening to music I don't feel;
Touching the ground with no answers
I want home.
Home,
I belong to where moon belongs.

6. My Morning Rose

You swipe the black ice
The fruits underneath
Bursting with sunlight,
Through the window
The kissed sun on your fragile skin,
And peeling grace biting into it
Would be the strewn dew of hope
And the sin of omission
You would understand that
preventing the fading of your
glinting hair is not
reflecting the beauty of the divine.
Your body was already
famous for its glory
Hours before you emerged
from the depth of stars.
From sunrise to sunset
executed with candles,
sights of my other side
watching your chimaeras.

7. Oceans of Her Own

I wish I could touch
I wish I could hug her
with my eyes open
and heart without chains
You were easy to talk
I couldn't see that time
how I was lucky
having you around
Your hands dusted sins of me
Touched my deep dim glow of fire
I wish I could touch
I wish I could hug her
with my eyes open
and heart without chains
You became distinct
a smoked song that hides inferno demons
shades to death
Why,
Why would this magic glow faint?
When we both were on the same sea
sinking in your heart , in your soul
was for me memories I was born with
I wish I could touch

I wish I could hug her
with my eyes open
and heart without chains
I wish I could have told her
All of this before the clouds reigned

8. I Tell You How You Broke Me

Poisoning my heart
with your fears
Your shadow that you couldn't heal
wasn't my deal
I have tried to save you
While you stabbed in my chest
I have tried to keep you
while you dusted my skin
My bones fleshed with scarfs
turned to tears and screams
Left for die on that cold floor
But my eyes kept trapped your selfish sight
I saw you leaving with sneaky look behind
Your demons smiled while my angels fallen
Your farewell pinched every meridian of mine
Sharpen blade thrown beside
my body couldn't talk
but my soul will never remain silent
Hush ! Whispered all the ghosts
You are now with one foot in ours
And the one kept on his collector's wall
of art and sour crafts.

9. Hopes And Lies

Hopes and lies,
Aren't they sisters
Playing, flirting all time together
Barely touching their skin?
Lies dance with hopes as smiles move
The hopes see only sources of joy.
Hopes never say words
And lies tell much
Hopes keep creating and inventing
With big innocent eyes enchanting
Dragging me out of matters
Pushing me to hug lies,
Even if see through her eyes the facts
Coincidences!
I never saw their realm
Or they are all dancing in destiny hall
where I get used to put my nose
What court could investigate in,
blame, or charge ?
Only me who believe in both
And show them the door of my own
Lies has been treated and contained
by thousands of years skills are shaped

Hopes feels sorry but can't be changed
As she was drawn by humans to fish their ferries
Could new generations walk off literally?
from all old lies and grid,
Transmitted and sustained all this time
Hope they will.

10. The Temple Of All Senses

Out of all lands, a dark green temple

Caught my prayers and all my soft senses

With only three large steps, to get in

and a large doors on wall

I entered the temple

And it took me courage to bring

All my dark snake skins,

My shadows and my old sins

On the journey,

I discovered some others,

sights and thoughts would creep

into my luggage and accompany me to there

The temple offered me a mirror

I saw a tall standing out silhouette

from the crowd brought me a crown

Dim faces in dark, I hear talking

They all had a room in my carry-on

but no more at the green temple

I had a little understanding

and clear explanation, shall be binding

I put down all my illusionary luggage

and kneeled for pray

I walked a miles away
and still felt the quietness of temple In me.

11. A Journey

A journey to happiness, is a journey to me
I start to put a smile,
then I draw a light
I opened that door, with a lantern in hand
I saw golden keys, live in fond
I took some keys and found they are all mine
I shook the jars and magic was seen
Stars came dancing, enchanted my body in a waltz scene
I laughed, and said that all is fine
Within me , all time is quite
That heart is real
and so all what's is around.

12. Earth with Women's Skin

I cry a mother who gives birth

To a son became, a leader

He forgets the womb who created him

That without, he couldn't be that right,

in eyes of others

who only shares air

With one finger, he ordered to throw stones

on her body, through her bones

Me, your mother,

A temple of God.

I cry a daughter who couldn't see the sunrise

upon her hair without any shames

plays with the winds and run like wolves

with broken thoughts, she can't go far

Borders, became a dome

Domesticated and buried underneath

on her knees she couldn't go so far

to see if dome was only an illusion

as a desired water, on the desert, or on road

She couldn't go so far

but her heart is wilder than the sky

And she created him again

Till Sun goes down
With the moon, she raised him
Singed for him dreams lullaby
Brought him pure food made of blood
She brought him to life, again
Even afterwards a rape
After a war that she never faced
On her grave they will write,
Finally,
Her name as her father gave.

13. Dead Poets

Dear poets are staring at me,

Waiting for me to talk

A speech which heals

With a voice of a lovers when they run to their dreams

With a voice of a lovers when they run from their faith

On that big table in front of me

I see, candles, yellow leafs,

feathers with a red ink stain

They blow-off some candles, and lighting up others

Asking me to burn myself with

Asking me to hear their call,

to feel their griefs,

to love hurting love, till I'll bleed destiny

I couldn't turn my face on,

something in me told me to beg them deeply

something in me told me to stay

Fearless than ever

I didn't see my life age turning the clock

I kept staring at them

I have even asked them to show me the old path,

so I can change mine

I have asked them to see with my eyes, so I can write the code

They smiled at me, they pushed what on that table only

Without any words, they told me, I am the chosen one,
to bear their heavy choices
to lights up candles and turn them off
for new lovers , childs , and lost souls
At the end I started the paths, cold and warm paths ,
distanced from me in the way I can still see
I took and carry what I could find on their table
with no smile yet on my face
but I know I'm happy already to find my way
I belong to this table, from many ages anyway
I never left dead poets table, and never will
I'll play with leafs, lights and griefs
so can see demons that I'll dance with
to distract them from lovers , Childs and lost souls.

14. Burning Mirror

Your kisses told me stories
Showed places,
where you want me to walk by
Places where I would never face storms and shadows, thought
I caught your breathing and hold it a while,
a moment, and the moment became a life
Stalks, growth makings its marks, felt was beautiful on me,
Felt I'm special enough to be by at your side
Then, a thorny brushes torn my dresses ,and then my skin
my face faded under your smiles
my shadow dim , looking for my shining side
and my walk never knew the come back way
You took my hand,
with slow walk down to the painted grave
Without a talk, I knew I was diving some unknown oceans
Wave after waves, you thought I was yours
Finally, your speaks adjusted with tunes
Told exactly who you are,
a past ghost coming from womb of beautiful art,
a framed washed by others rain
A women who cares about her son,
but the sun became streets slaves
I thought my bright will change his sights

and after,
I left his book of stories to look for myself
his whispers kept chasing me
but his kisses never last.
There, no victims was
only two people who saw the different side of the mirror .
one see fire , when other see light
Burning mirror
Burning mirror with two sides
Burning mirror
Your kisses told me stories,
Show places where you want me to walk,
places where I would never face storms and shadows ,
I caught your breathing and hold it a while, a moment,
The moment became a life
Stalks, growth making its marks,
Felt was beautiful on me,
felt I'm special enough to be by your side
But a thorny brushes torn my frocks, then my skin
My face faded under your smiles
My shadow dim , looking for my shining side
and my walk never knew the comeback home
you took my hand , with slow walk down to the painted grave
Without a talk , I knew I was diving some unknown oceans
Wave after wave, you thought I was yours
Finally your words adjusted with tunes
told exactly who you are ,

a past ghost coming from womb of beautiful art,

a framed washed by others rain

a women who cares about her son ,

but the sun became streets slaves

I thought my bright will change his sights

and after ,

I left his book of stories to look for myself

his whispers kept chasing me

but his kisses never last.

There, no victim was

but only two people who saw the different side of the mirror

One sees the fire , when other sees the light

Burning mirror

its marks , felt was beautiful on me ,

felt I'm special enough to be by your side

but a thorny brushes torn my dresses, a then my skin too

my face faded under your smiles

my shadow dim , looking for my shining side

and my walk never knew the come back way

you took my hand , with slow walk down to the painted grave

without a talk , I knew you were diving me to some unknown

oceans

wave after waves , you thought I was yours,

and you washed all my hopes

Finally then, your words adjusted with tunes

You told me, exactly, who you are

A past ghost coming from womb

of beautiful art,

as a framed washed by others rain

A simple women , mother, who cares about her son,

but her son became streets slaves , and sold his soul

I thought my bright will change his sights she said

I thought my love will dust off my memories, I said.

And after ,

His whispers kept chasing me

His kisses never last.

I left his book,

and I closed the door behind.

There, no victim was

But only two people who saw the different side of the mirror .

One still sees fire, when others see only truths.

15. Demons

What if intimidating demons was a foul game?
Speaking what's in one's heart is a labyrinth shrinking at any
turn,
showing a coming back home.
Leaving others'seen truth will make my wings freeze
What if dancing with,
reveals my roots and
singing with,
aches my skins to new
What if they can't hear my laugh,
no more
What if demons don't wear black
Spreads flowers and kills the fears
What if their beauty is divine
Wasn't created by same light ?
What if their houses are infinite seas
What if their fire was only sun light
What if their skies are dark so we can see stars
What if their drums were only our dying hearts
What if they were through hell, with us
Prepared us frankly
I'm not scare any more.

16. Incarnation

Why don't we live forever?
Live like we know it all.
Digging into the depth of our hearts,
will never surprise us.
Come
Come, take my hand,
and breathe in the stardust that we belong to.
Stay beside me
like we've known each other for a long time now
Reach for my intention, no blames, no lies,
so you'll know how to pick me up when I'm down,
Because I know I'll do the same for you.
If my heart bleeds,
you will smile and tell me with your eyes,
that everything will be fine.
Let's wear white
and let colours dance around;
let's tell them that the light we have been looking for
all those years,
is inside while the dark is out there.
We will laugh together like children and say:
"without the night we can't see the beauty of the stars"
Let's travel through oceans,

reach out to seas,

and wave to the lands up there

Bring me that breath that I've been longing for to feel alive…

to feel Alive,

Stars dust,

We are the dust of stars.

17. In White Dress Actress

Everybody wants her,
The whole world wants to know,
what it would feel like to be "Her"
She always felts alone
She was real, and out of everyone's league
The face of an angel who lost her wings
Everyone picked a feather from "Her"
to have the magical moment,
of feeling close to her
She started to feel her wings weighing her down
As she passes by a dark streets,
and looks through windows of families
gathering or fighting.
She tooks off her paired coracoid
The flame of her white candle flickers dyingly.
She prayed for her young face to last forever
and the legend turned out to became true.
We see her eternal beauty,
still untouchable,
Her walk became as famous
as A Marilyn Monroe's.
They want her shadow

So they got her wings.

She used to be a pale white

They covered her skin,

with chalk dust

She has been drawn

She started to feel her wings weighing her down

as she was passing by a dark streets,

and looks through windows of others houses.

She took off her paired coracoid

So the flame of her white candle flickers dyingly.

She prayed for her young face to last forever

So the legend turned out to live forever.

We see her eternal beauty,

still on walls hanging,

Her walk became famous

Known by lovers.

By women dreams

You look down and I understand that

The magic was Her

and the rest,

are a shadow holders.

18. Broken Bones

You poison my heart
With your fears, and
your shadows that you couldn't heal.
That wasn't the deal.
I tried to save you,
while you were busy stabbing my chest.
I tried to keep you,
while you were busy dusting my skin.
My bones fleshed with scars
Turned into tears and screams.
Abandoned for death
on that cold floor, I Was
But my eyes were trapped in your selfish sight.
I saw you leaving with a final sneaky look behind,
your demons smiled
while my angels fallen.
Your walking farewell pinched every meridian of mine.
You sharpen blade thrown beside
my body. I couldn't talk
But, my soul will never remain silent.
Hush, whispered all the ghosts
you are now, with one foot in our world
I said :

And the other one on this collector's wall
hanged
Art's walls, of and sour crafts, he said.

19. Apocalypse

The children of new earth is birthing
They are here
Breathing
Learning
Teaching, and showing
different lives,
different love.
They're light;
They're not us;
They're playing;
They're dancing;
They're proving that we were once
Broken thoughts, and
broken hearts are
After magic was killed
and replaced by walls;
and nature replaced by wars.
They see things we can't understand;
They speak a language, we hear songs.
They scare old soldiers,
Old laws and skies.
With their hands,
They grow trees and plants.

They are here
With our faces,
Bodies and veins;
But not with our walk,
that we thought was a fall.
They are time without chains;
Time without hours or minutes.
They talk to the stars
and sleep in the dark naked
They're here,
They're now
And alive.

20. I Am Leaving You

Temporary…temporary.
Everything is ephemeral in my hands
It moves too fast or too slow,
domesticated between my thoughts and my prayers
I can barely grab a dusted scent,
memories,
voices that were alive once,
friends or family members
run-in and clame
A Vanished hugs
A twisted kisses
A heart of Acid and insoluble ashes.

21. A Journey With ME

In a wooden chalet, I was
With crackling fire narrating my story.
If only I knew how to unravel mysteries.
Hand against a window, a winter scenery
I saw snowing flakes, and ghosts behind trees.
The fire of zeal taught me things
while I was thirsting after myths,
from others books,
with my wand on hand
pulling out the invisible words
of virgins feelings.
The cold old water river flows,
gathered from tears
towards oceans, lakes, or seas.
We all know and comprehend
that it is our nature ,Supreme, who guides
Tell us with wisdom and knowledge stirred…
Except the wind…
Which danced in slightly sacred movements
I was lying on the ground
Looking at those movements,
as a reflection of flames on a ceiling
Of blaze or of a setting sun.

Blessed eyes!, I said.
I witnessed, in the silence of night,
Melodies singing my loneliness
Kept enchanting my ears;
Heartbeats,
Were my only loyal partners.
In the chalet, there was
Only me, myself, and my dreams
the future once, and the moment I seek.
If only I knew how to be present
leave the unpacked memories…
If only I stayed in the chalet
With my heart, that fire,
and my only main steering.

22. Your Eyes

Beyond the chains,
Beyond the end,
I can see future;
I can touch the horizon.
Oceans are drops;
Grasslands deserted,
and only you in frame.
Your shadows are my day life,
And my night slippers are,
Your eyes
Always be your eyes.

23. If I Died Yesterday

Temporary, temporary…
Everything is ephemeral in my hands
It moves too fast, or too slow
Domesticated between my thoughts and prayers.
I can barley grab from a dusty scene
A scent and memories,
Voices that have once been alive,
Friends or family members,
My time and my lovers…
I hear my heart beat, knocking
on my minds doors
To wake me up
To shake me up
If I feel cold,
Then I still feel, still…
I can't move
But I will.
All my senses,
are screaming my given name.
I asked them to wait;
A nighte, a year , or an eternity
I'm hearing all about
In this world, and the others.

24. Light Queens

Dark and light queens
One night switched their castles.
In one, there were healers
In the other, spells.
Wines and ear rye.
Raise from skulls
In prayer hands.
Wolves and fairies
In praying hands;
Moon and sun
And a skyline in between,
Curves touching shadows.
Glowing skins are shining
In mediaeval dresses
Or naked remains,
Both are dancing
In waves and Graves.
Moon queen
said *we are light;*
we die each time you shine
the Sun queen responded
we are yet the universe's heart.
We will keep each other warm.

25. Dear Old Me

The past is calling me secretly

At night,

When it's too quiet

When I'm alone, always

If I don't answer, I wonder

Lessons around could be dismissed

Questions standing,

Looking straight at me

Waiting for the dance, and the step moves

Hopes bridges made of paper

Reflecting fragility of glasses below

Faded distance between us

And two strong hands keeping me on hold

One for faith one for love

So far I distinguished

Keepers of my skills laughing

With golden keys on the chest

Shadows of my past hunting my present

With two wild open doors

One with love smooth and gentle fresh wind

With angel voices singing love

One with regrets strangle my breath, to death

With demons smiling

Things that couldn't happen
and would not
and I'm in the middle with my parents stories, that can't help
after reading my poem, You answered:
I feel the Poem
With love, I Sent:
The past is calling , again
He couldn't find me where I was left,
anymore
Standing with a sword
Looking behind
Echoed stepping back of his own shadows,
he could only find
That past , I created ,
Was my life coach in act.

26. And You Dare!

What "Better" means to you,
Is not what I can see?
We are only in different spaces
Different sees
Cold water for you
Is little happiness shaking waves, for me
Hot weather for you
Is sunny day for me
Clouds and grey days for you
Are a changing energies
That I welcome with dances
I'm not different, I'm not "Better"
I'm just standing,
in different spaces of souls

27. You Came Back

I don't want to live in your dreams
I want to be next to you, living
because once we are dead
Angels will ask, where did I spend my heart?
I want other answer than,
In his dreams
I am not your fantasy
Sinking in your unbarring past and now
I'm flesh, bones and hearts
Moods and fails
I'm a whole, and all hanging words,
Fallen from the skies.

28. Yes, That Simple

Yes, That Simple
Happiness!
My Happiness!
Doesn't need miracle
Extraordinary visions
It doesn't need crowd clapping
Sometimes it's woven with a Stanger smile
A classic black and white Polaroids frames.
Sometimes it came as a song
Hums in a silly note of a passenger a cross the road
Sometimes it's changed kisses of birds, on a branches
Or a dispute of them for a little of space
That we think is a lovers conversation
My happiness is found in simple things
that universe tries to offer in ways we can't see
A Goosebumps form
A hand on chest breathing
A calm sundown kissing our sights
Agitated night with calm dark sky
Decorated with memories of stars
In old letter found in old wood box
Old baby choes
or my Old childhood choes

Trying to reminds me of little things
That I thought forget
Jumping under hot sunny days
An open mouth testing first tears of winter clouds
An old school book with some silly sketches, and weird words
A jumping rope left on sidewalk
A small home with big windows
And vanilla cookies smells, after a long day.

29. Emerged War

I took a refuge in your heart
Thought was for a lifetime
What if your lifetime is short?
or longer than mine!
I took a refuge in your heart
For a lifetime
In a heart screaming slef-seeking,
With no doors or windows open.
I've tried to paint,
a burned heart
A burning heart loves the fire
I have tried to paint my broken arms
Broken arms are warmest when hugging
Those stuck in time are,
those who missing a person
with a wilted flowers
Hearing voices saying:
Lemon squeezed upon eyes, seeing truth now how it was drawn

30. Unjustified oceans

Creatures calling deaths of all lives
Essences coming out all dark waves
Talking about love
and decimate all wrong behaviours
A blooming theatre
for deaf and blind spectators
Our world is,
All our mistakes and wishes
In one rope.

31. Can You See My Heart?

I am radiating such light

But I don't blind people

When I let my feet kiss the ground

And my eyes hug the skyline

I can hear the Sun whispering to my soul

Words that we all want to hear

When I let breath my heart

I can see the clouds drawing and talking to my inner child

Then, a soft smile shows up without a call

I told to myself, today, is a good day to just Live

Live

Yes, just live.

Today I will not sail with my thoughts

I have decided so

I will shine and let my soul take Queen Chair

I am radiating my real light

Without making people blind

32. A Note To Self!

One day you will look back
Looking, where you did put the dark
At the Aura River you will find
She wrote:
One day you will ask, why?
You listened to your heart?
Followed ghosts?
Dreamed about perfection?
Your heart teached you life
She wrote:
One day
That day you will kiss your lips on the mirror.
Feel the dry, cracked lips,
of an old body
No winter on it , only four season
You'll caressing them gently
The time caused
She wrote,
One day
No fire will burn you
No void will shakes you
No memories will freeze you
She wrote,

Now you read this

You know the right door to open

To follow

To pull towards oneself

The view you will not share

The light flame of her wings

You see!

She wrote...

33. I Can See You

Can I ask you, my dear, my friend
All secrets that you hold, deep inside
Can I have?
Your cherry lips to kiss mine
Can I ask you?
If your heart could be mine
For one day
For one night
For one of my thousand dreams
Where should I sit?
To just stare at you
No words to say
What should I tell
or not tell ,
about you
to myself.
Can I ask you
To hold me tight
So my whispers flow
Through your ears, hair
Softly

34. Lost Land

How the sun doesn't nourish them,
but the moon causes the sap to rise
Trees against the sky
Tall
Castle without walls
Colours as we never could see
Art and wine
Creatures are all same
With noble heart and light inside

35. To The Rabbit Lover

I wrote it for a friend here,
He asked the universe
And universe answered
Named him " Sacred Love"
I have been searching for you
Sacred Love
My entire life, and in-between
When I am alone
When I am lost
When I write a few words
To Hunt, fish or trap you
I have been searching for you
My friend, if I may!
My idol, if you existed
I have been searching for you
Sacred love
For centuries
In love stories, books and short talks
In fantastic maps
Through dark lane
I have heard you laughing
In sound of stepping dancer
Through a sight or under makeup of strangers

Or a light voice of an attractive woman
Through a bride in her pure dresses
Through a mother who gives birth
Screaming life, so skies could pray
I have been searching for you
Through highest mountains
To the deepest thoughts of detained
I have been searching for you
Through an orphan,
While looking up to the billions of stars
I have been searching
And will
till my next life
Under or above skies.

36. Unchained Believes

She is smoking freedom
So close to my chest
She is breathing, learning
Teaching herself again
She is talking tango moves
Explaining herself by fairy morse
Like an Owl in dark skies
She is screaming her glory
Attempting the hard version of her
Creating lives on her womb
Metamorphic the divine body
For bringing the world's immortal humans
An Angel who loves
And wear a demon fancy dance.

37. The Dream

Frozen in the past
Where my childhood belongs
Sugar, senses, magic and plays
They have asked me to learn
But they didn't show me how to suffer
They have asked me to win
But they didn't show me how to fail
They have asked me to sing
Melody that doesn't have notes
They played wars
Conquered continents
Killed, replaced
How?
How could I survive without a centre of universe
How could I not follow my heart
Speaking the truth
See the unseen
Draw and breath
How could light be blind
Burn the water,
and steam off the road
How
How do I leave the doors closed?

To a stranger who can't believe
That Love is the keys

38. A Journey

The journey from me to myself
Cutting roots hurted me most
Drinking dark water and get lost
Between past and layers of ancient lives
Was rough
In tumultuous ways
I met
Versions of Virgins with spouse faces
A blind lords judging
A blood keeper smiling
A ghost and demons singing
Swans in muds dancing
Witches without homes
Wizards without cone
A deaf mute teachers playing on ground
In tumultuous truth
I saw
The unseen and the untold
Secrets with millions swords
Cutting times of laws
I saw
A wise man jokes with troubadours
A circuses without sources

I went to meet the moon
To learn how to become beasts tamer
To fly with wind
And talk to the fire
The moon teached me one thing
to look deep at traveller soul
I turned my face and said to the clarity
I mean, to half domed rising sun
Duality, can't balance and never will
On places where only Me can reigns

39. Owns Less?

Gold
Because it belongs to mountains and caves
The womb of earth
Air
Because it belongs to Skies and winds
Hands of changes
Love
Because it belongs to lovers
Who nevertheless will meet?
Courage
Because it belongs to demons
Who dare to decide?
Loneliness
Because I belong to the whole
And whole is linked to the one
Life
Because it belongs to death
When it came in steps of the dancing time
I am Ownerless
With Losses, indeed
Independent and free
That's how to be

40. The Wood Spirit

I felt you catching my lungs
Cutting my hair
Singing, breathing
Putting my faith in mud
Blind my pas was
Spirit woods Sais:
Breath, breath

41. I Think

I Think
I think I meant to live differently
See things unlikely
Feel things by the soul
When others are amazed by sunset
I see reflection of it in their eyes
On the leafs and feathers
Those talk to be more than the rest
I think I meant to live differently

42. Forced

Forced to live again
Reincarnated in total unknown
Trying to understand who am i
Only to meet you again
That is the curs to love you forever
Or disclose into oblivion forever shall

43. Love

Love!

Is it a curse?

I start believing the story of Adam and Eve

Is a lie!

Something happened then

That no one wants to remember…

44. It Was Not Mine

You made my smiles and sights
Nourished by your ideas
Even if it was not mine
A thirsty sapiophile devouring each second
As it was eternal
Staring your words painting my existence
For a solemn moment, for a while
A constellation that I cannot feign

45. Live

Being passionate will curse you to live,
live life in most beautiful way
Live , fully, unconditionally & deeply

46. I Don't

I don't smell like flowers
because they are tender and soft
I smell wild dreams
that you can never get
I smell Love & hates
bouncing up all your desires

47. Mirror

Mirror Mirror
passion has broken my whole
my heart felt for a stranger
with no home , no town
only a face to remember
with a sour regret and my temper
and a living embers
Mirror Mirror
cast that spell
I'm no longer faithful to my anger
that caused my pain

48. Fearing Love

I ran
fearing Love
I ran
to my insignificant routine
telling myself lies forced to believe
I ran

49. False Goodness

I crossed my heart with Lucifer's swords
Burning with billions of years flames
An insatiable desire of belonging
To whom preaching day and night their false goodness.

50. Exhuasted Passion

My exhausted passion
facing a blank frame
wondering how the colours
will tell my tells!

51. Seen

I have been drinking from universes
Sucking stars and sculpting my thoughts

52. Wholeness

My body is a whole story
A valley of tenderness
Where flowers in each season bloom
And if you want to reach their mountains,
You have no clue
My rivers saturated, un-breathable
Wholeness
A chemistry of all possible melodies
Well preserved in a doomed existence

53. Don't Fall in Love

Don't,

Don't fall in love with a woman who loves poetry,

And tell enchanting story

Don't,

You will only be lost…

54. I Answsered

He said once:
"I do not like you"
So, you do not like art,
I answered.

55. Ancestors

Sepiternal sadness
of our ancestors
Blaming,
Ashamed calling
Our ancestors to break circles.

56. Who Would Count?

Who could count his walking steps
From the day of birth, making steps
I have walked for so many years
My words would say
In mommy sheets thoughts will plead
An overnight my dreams would play
And another day my heart would stay.

57. Dances

Dances !
Oh they are prayers too
In a form of loving itself
With speed of sound,
With rhythms flow

58. Innocent Eyes

If my hands could force time to flee
Capture those moments & return them to me
My smiles & innocent eyes,
My heart flying like a bee
From flower to flower I can be
If my knees don't shake
Jumping hopscotch free
Sonic pulse waving laugh
Drumming heavy in my ears caught

59. Greedy Heart

Porcelain flowers
Counting hours
On chef blooming
In hand of a greedy heart

60. Forbidden Fruits

We are children of the forbidden fruits
We are not children of Abel, no
We will forever disputing survival
Territories creating,
genders and ethnicity giving approval
We only can imagine
Hope dancing tiptoes in front of blindly humans,
And clapping for deaf

61. Better Late Than Never

An opsymath in life mistaken
Onslaught memories forsaken
One foot dance with love
another with the forgotten
we all will say :
Better late than never

Chapter62

Dear reader write Your feedback, love and valuable commments here............